1 2 3 4 5

6 2 8 9 10

Hungry For Numbers

Etienne Delessert

CREATIVE EDITIONS

MANKATO, MINNESOTA

1

one banana

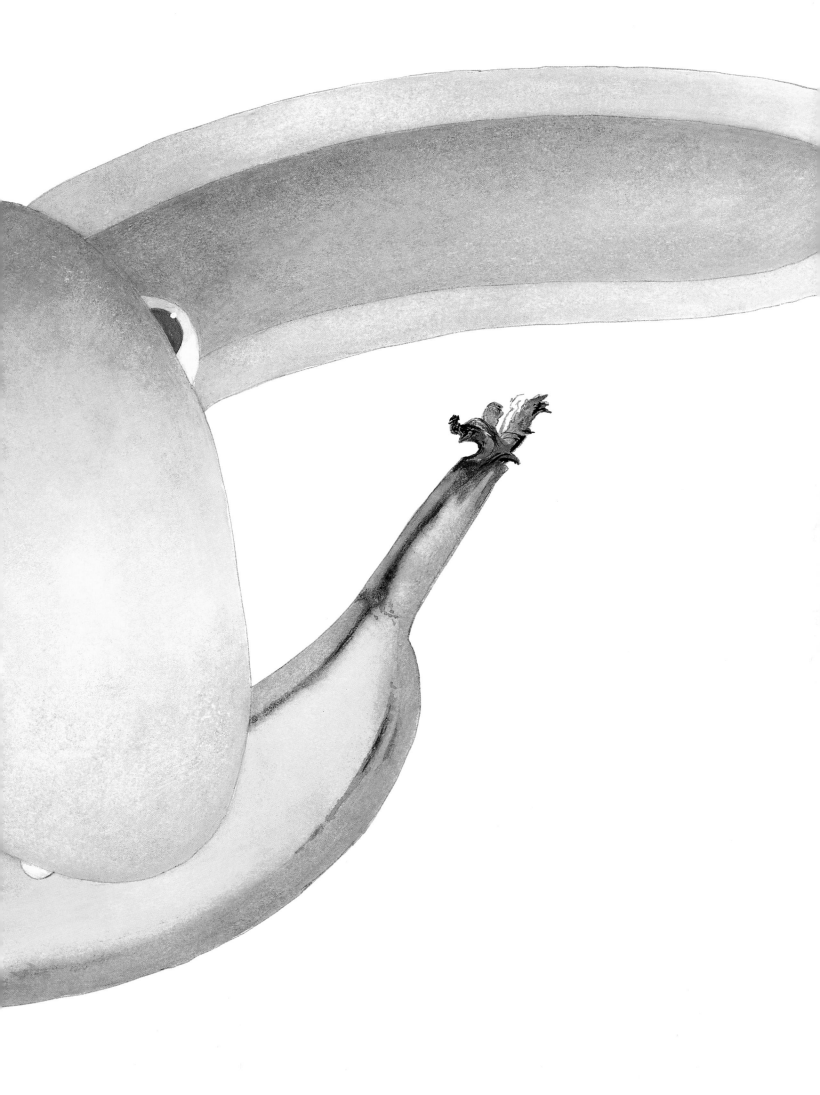

2
two apples

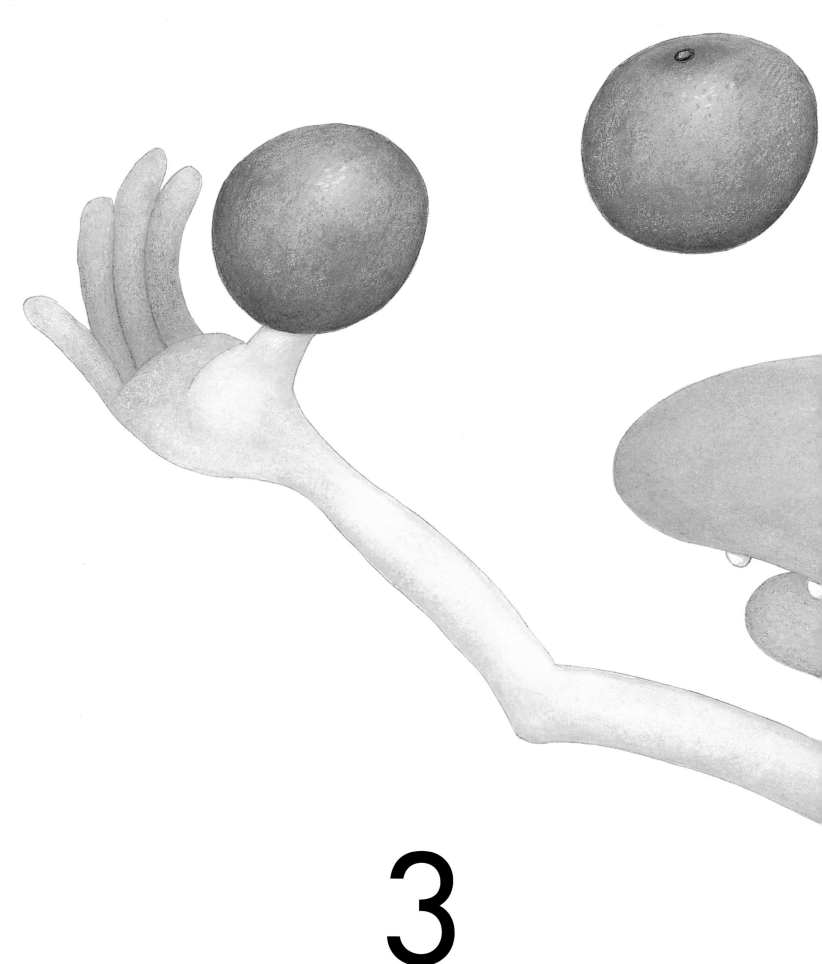

3

three oranges

4

four cherries

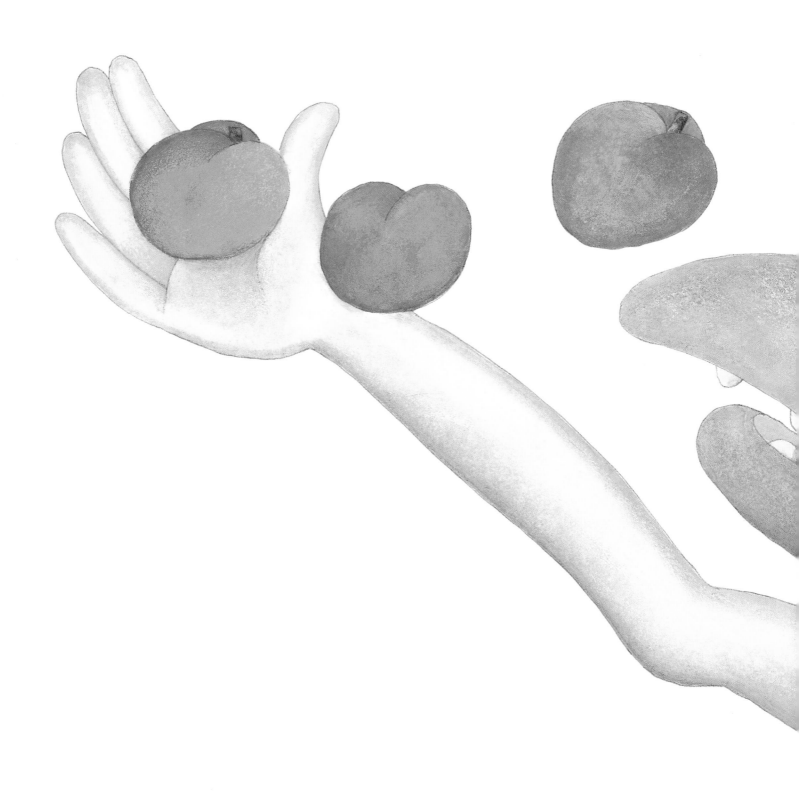

5

five apricots

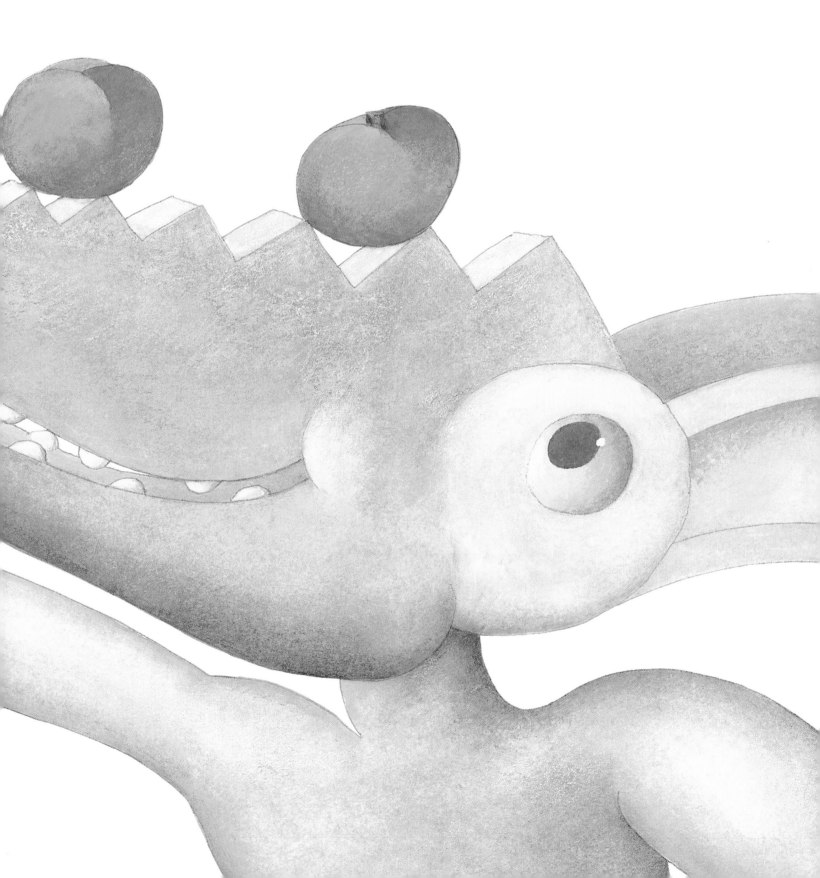

6

six plums

7

seven strawberries

8
eight peaches

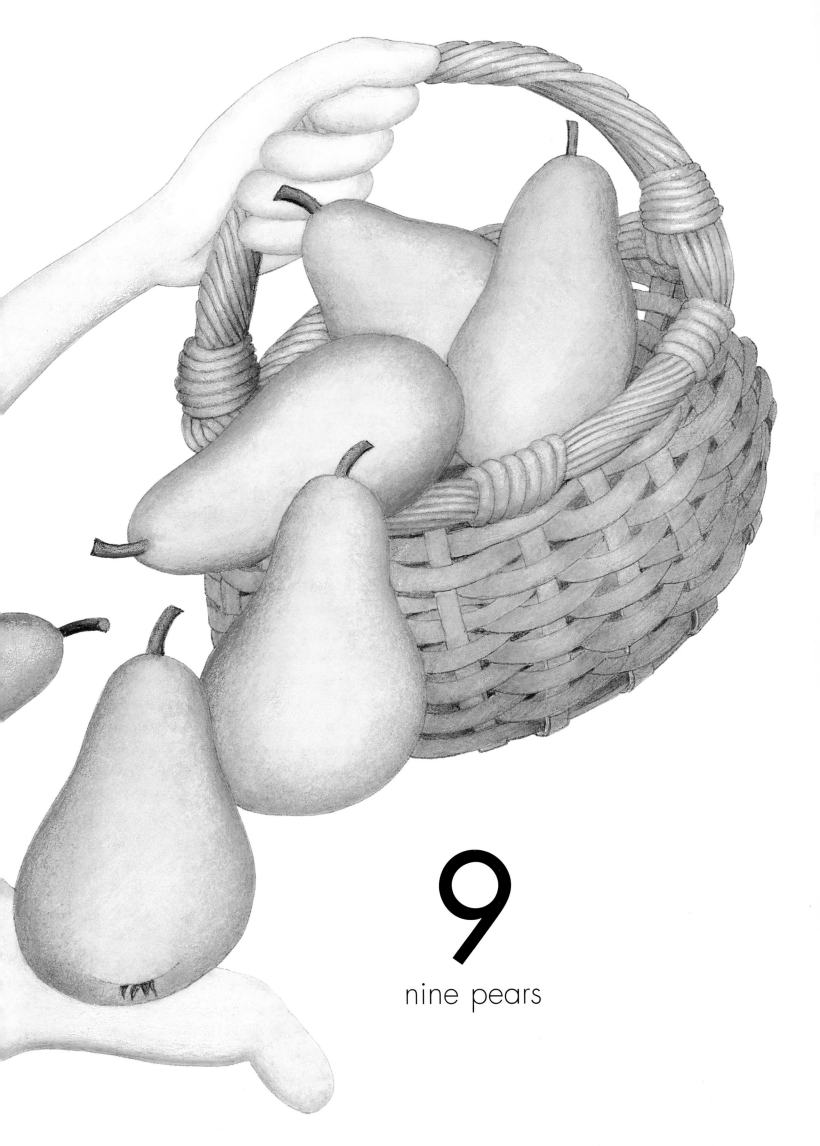

9

nine pears

10

ten blueberries

What fun!

1 2 3 4 5

one　　two　　three　　four　　five

6 7 8 9 10

six   seven   eight   nine   ten

Ilustrations copyright © 2006 Etienne Delessert

English translation copyright © 2006 Creative Editions

Published in 2006 by Creative Editions

123 South Broad Street, Mankato, MN 56001 USA

Creative Editions is an imprint of The Creative Company.

Text and illustrations copyright © 2005 Gallimard Jeunesse

First published in 2005 by Gallimard Jeunesse,

Le goût des chiffres, as part of an anthology entitled Jeux d'en-

fant.

Designed by Rita Marshall

Printed in Italy

Library of Congress Cataloging-in-Publication Data

Delessert, Etienne.

Hungry for Numbers / [illustrated by] Etienne Delessert.

ISBN 1-56846-196-8

1. English language—Alphabet—Juvenile literature. I. Title.

PE1155.D445 2005

428.1—dc22   2004061174Light

First Edition 5 4 3 2 1